How I Brought Good from a Bad Online Publishing Experience

Creating Positive Outcomes from Negative Writing Gigs & Avoiding Them

By: James M. Lowrance © 2012

TABLE OF HEADINGS:

INTRODUCTION:

This is now my third short subject book, regarding a negative publishing experience I have had on the World Wide Web, that I was eventually able to glean positive things from. While I have written about other similar experiences in past books, this is my first time for relating this particular one. I will not be referring to any websites by name, as I provide some details regarding my experience.

There are many writers for content websites and those who are publishing their self-authored eBooks who have at-times, experienced the bad side of dealing with online business entities, just as I have. For many, this can result in them putting a halt to their efforts in attempting to publish successfully because they literally feel as if they have hit a wall that hinders their ability to grow as aspiring writers. This is especially true when they have several bad experiences with e-commerce publishing companies, which can leave them with a bad impression in-general, toward businesses that are within this field.

4

It is my opinion however, that just about any negative online experience in publishing, can present positive possibilities and certainly not all publishing opportunities are potentially negative because many have great potential and are offered by highly ethical companies. With this said, it sometimes requires honest-but-shrewd thinking and a determination to move forward regardless of any setbacks that might be experienced by developing authors.

Much of what I will relate within the headings that follow is in regard to a content website I previously wrote for that is actually reputable and that does display a high level of online quality. My experience with the site CEO/owner does not necessarily detract from the aspects they have gained toward positive online presence.

It does however, demonstrate the fact that authors/writers who contribute to them, are not always recognized for the essential part they may play in building and sustaining their visitor-traffic via their published articles.

When content contributors recognize a downward trend in treatment from the administration of websites they enter into contract with, they should seriously consider taking some degree of action to overcome it, as an obstacle to their own growth as authors. Over time, this can make a difference within the field of content websites in-general, who should be willing to offer contracts/agreements that are reasonably beneficial to writers and treatment toward them that is reasonably fair for their hard work.

Certainly content websites should also protect their own interests and should be recognized for having the authority to correct their contract contributors and to also reprimand them when it becomes necessary.

If such a relationship becomes unreasonably imbalanced in the favor of either party, the slighted party should be prepared to seek resolution to the problem. In-short, I believe it is important for sincere writers to move forward from negative experiences they may have in regard to online publishing, which is the subject of this book.

It is my sincere hope that the personal experience I relate within the headings that follow and the advice I add to my related experience, will offer a bit of positive inspiration to my fellow online publishers, who are simply seeking to enter into honest relationships with ethical e-commerce companies.

-Jim Lowrance

1. My First Experience as an Editor for a High Traffic Website

Early in the year 2008, I applied to become a topic editor for a high traffic, multi-topic content website, where I would also serve as editor of the forum that would also fall under the topic I would be covering for the site. This would hold considerable responsibility and the compensation would not be a revenue share of ad income or a salary but would rather be a "promotional opportunity", in which editors for the site could gain writing experience and be allowed to place affiliate links under each of their articles. This could be links to a company the editor was selling a product for or it could be a product being offered directly by the editor, such as some type of consumer product or even an eBook or paperback book they have authored. The site also offered training for the editor position, which included optional courses on subjects such as eBook formatting and promotion. The ongoing training was also a benefit because practice in writing, brings improved skills and quality toward the future content produced by an aspiring author/editor.

I was working full time employment at the time I began my online writing pursuit and so I wasn't actually looking for a paying online writing job but rather one for which I could grow my writing abilities and offer online content to readers that would be genuinely helpful to them. The fact that I was not actually seeking pay for my content was also evident in the fact that I had written several dozen articles for this same topic at this website as a "guest author", going back to the year 2005. The previous editor was happy to include my content after I contacted her, offering to submit articles for consideration. After a period of time, this editor would actually begin writing to me, requesting new articles for the site-topic and I was always happy to oblige. This familiarity with the website, was the reason I applied for the editor position, once it was resigned by the previous editor who decided that the position demanded a bit too much of her time in exchange for a limited amount of promotion but for no actual monetary compensation. Even with this fact in mind, I was eager to step into the position, once the website placement team for editors contacted me in follow-up to my application.

2. A Misspelling in the Same Article that Granted Me Editorship

They let me know that I would have to submit an article, as a final stage of consideration to be accepted for the position, that would need to be on the subject of the topic I would become editor for, pending approval. I was happy to write the article and to send it to them, which was on the topic-subject as they requested but I wrote it from the perspective of its relationship to the highly famous celebrity -- Oprah Winfrey. As a result of the submitted article, they sent me a final approval notice to fill the vacant editor position. I was also informed that I would be undergoing a 3 month training course, so that I was familiar with the site's publishing tools and to be well-informed regarding copyright law, HTML coding, etc... The multi-subject course would provide me the education I would need to effectively fulfill my duties as the new editor and I completed it, within the period of time required by them (actually ahead of schedule).

I began to publish articles on the site, right away and I faithfully answered posts being made on the accompanying forum, promptly as I saw them coming in.

I was enjoying the work and my intention was to continue with the position indefinitely. At one point I published the same article for the website topic that included information about Oprah Winfrey within it. This was the same article that I had submitted as a final stage of my application to the site, weeks earlier that resulted in my approval for the position. This article had been running live for a couple of months, when the site owner -- the CEO who was overseeing activity on this content entity, contacted me to let me know that I had misspelled Oprah Winfrey's name. She found where I rendered the spelling within the article, as "Ophra", rather than the correct "Oprah"; the incorrect spelling being my placing of the "h", after the "p", rather than it falling at the end of her name where it needed to be. It amazed me that this mistake was not caught by the editor placement people, so they apparently were not clear on the correct spelling either.

3. A Legitimate Correction Request with an Insulting Attitude

I did not mind being notified about this error; in fact I wanted to be contacted about any issues of this type so that I could correct them appropriately. This would help my topic on the site to remain the best quality possible. What was concerning to me, was the way in which the site owner approached the notification she directed to me. Within the corrective email, she added "You would think that this would be something you would want to get right!" This was basically an insulting notification regarding the error, rather than being a business-like request for correction. I immediately went into the article and made the correction at each point where Oprah's name was mentioned. I also wrote to the site owner, informing her that I made the correction. I explained to her, that I had originally searched for the correct spelling and found a discussion on a major bookseller forum, in which consumers were discussing one of Oprah's books. They spelled her name "Ophra" and I went with that incorrect rendering, rather than confirming its accuracy with several online sources (a mistake I learned from).

The site owner/CEO added more insult to her earlier correction by replying to my email with a statement saying "Any 13 year old child can find a name spelling the way you did." She did follow that remark by informing me about how she searched for name spellings online but this did not take away from the biting remarks that preceded the advice. Amazingly, toward the end of her email, she actually misspelled Oprah Winfrey's last name, by leaving the "e" off of it! In light of the sharpness found in some of her "corrective advice", I made a short reply, telling her that it would never happen again but I also highlighted her own misspelling in yellow, without actually pointing it out to her. I knew she would see my highlight and I hoped it would make the point that mistakes do occasionally happen but ones like these are not worthy of a corrective insult or of a reprimand.

4. When Unnecessary Venting Takes Over Professional Etiquette

I probably shouldn't have highlighted the site owner's misspelling but I felt her emails to me contained words that were uncalled for. I was after all, contributing a lot of articles to the topic, for "zero" monetary compensation and I had been contributing content for at least two years previous to becoming an editor and this was the gratitude I was shown in return for my volunteered work. I actually wondered if possibly something in this website CEO's personal life, was causing her to be unduly unkind to the very people who were making her website successful and to generally work well on the web, by venting unrelated frustrations toward them. With the fact that the site was advertised as a source for women, in spite of having many male editors, I also wondered if there might be a degree of gender bias involved or that I had possibly insulted a female hero of hers, by misspelling her name. I really had no idea for certain what was eating at this individual but I did know beyond even a small doubt, that her editor correction measures were highly unbalanced -- at least toward me.

If this were simply my opinion, then one might say that I was being overly-sensitive however; I showed the correspondence sent to me by the site CEO, to several other people who immediately saw the same thing I did -- namely, an overboard and insulting response to request correction for my name-spelling error.

I moved forward and decided to place the incident behind me but I would find (likely due to my pointing out her own misspelling mistake) that the site owner would never from that point forward, acknowledge any appreciation for me and she would not address me by name in her business emails that were in reply to specific site-related inquiries from me.

If for example, I had to report an issue that was occurring with the site's publishing tools, the site owner would respond to me, with a reply that made no mention of my name at the front of it (no salutation of any kind) and she would simply add her name at the bottom, with no actual sign-off (i.e. no "Sincerely", "Thank You", "Best Wishes" or "Regards", etc...).

After a period of time seeing this, I sent a letter to resign the topic editor position and I specifically described the issues that led to my resignation. This included the overboard correction-request that was directed at me for the Oprah Winfrey name misspelling.

5. Basic Standards in Business Practice are Obvious (No Surveys Required)

The site owner wrote me back with a reply, basically stating that it was no skin off her nose if I wanted to resign the editorship (the intended message: "good riddance"). She also found it ridiculous that I expected her to run her business, with business-like conduct; namely, the addressing of email recipients by name. I replied with links to several business etiquette websites, in which it was specifically stated that emails within a company should always include a salutation, using the recipient's name. She replied to this suggestion that I backed with reputable business advice websites, by saying that she had inquired with several other editors at the website as a result of my email, asking them if they wanted to be addressed by name and her report to me on this inquiry/survey was to say that these editors found the suggestion to be humorous and that they did not care to be addressed by name -- the implication being, that I was expecting something ridiculous in regard to email communications.

If this is actually the case and these editors did indeed inform the site owner with this type of answer regarding no need for their name recognition, then I would wonder why they either have no respect for their selves or why they would not care if anyone else does either? Surely the site had more quality types of individuals serving as editors than was implied by the CEO's purported answer to the inquiry/survey. My suspicion is that no such inquiry was ever actually made and that the site CEO simply wanted her improper business stance to appear to have merit, when it obviously didn't. The term "saving face" comes to mind in regard to her claims regarding the very impersonal business email communications methods. Some people, who are working within similar online businesses, would literally see this type of business ethic, as simply being lazy, disrespectful and seriously lacking quality.

6. The Apple Doesn't Fall Far from the Tree

I would also mention that it took the site more than two years from the time of my resignation, for them to fill the editor position. The person who did fill the editorship spot for the topic, apparently holds to the same level of business ethic that the site CEO does because after I sent her several eBooks on the same subject as the site-topic to review as a promotion exchange, she did not follow-through with the reviews nor respond to me in any way (I planned to return a promotion to this editor, by helping her to publish through book/eBook venues, which was yet to be fully discussed).

After I emailed her the eBooks, which she requested from me in answer to an earlier email I sent her, she simply never responded and now many months later, I do not expect a response. Her silence was not due to a dislike for my written works because she had previously complimented my authored articles, all of which the website continued to carry for two years following my resignation and many still appear there at the time of this writing as well.

Another reason I remained connected in-a-sense to the website in addition to my articles remaining live there, was due to my receiving a newsletter from them, that I remained signed-up for. While there was bad blood so-to-speak, between the site CEO and me, this did not take way from the fact that the specific topic was one of ongoing importance to me, plus I did not expect a future editor to also be at odds with me. It is possible that the new editor received negative feedback regarding me, from the site CEO. I felt however, that I was entitled at least to the free newsletter, in light of the fact that my articles have remained on their site for an extended period of time and I never requested removal of them. Apparently my articles were good enough for them to continue running live, in spite of my resigning the editorship for the reasons I did.

7. The Dark Cloud with the Silver Lining

As is the case with many people who experience similar scenarios, I could have simply thrown my hands up in the air as a result of them and walked away from online publishing forever.

What positive outcomes could I have possibly taken from this somewhat negative experience with the multi-topic content website? There are actually several positive things I have gleaned from the experience, in spite of the negative behaviors I was on the receiving end of. First of all, I was able to work on my writing skills during my period of time as an editor for them.

I learned better, how to space paragraphs for readers so that they didn't feel there were too many extended blocks of information within my articles. I also improved my grammatical methods, my punctuation and my sentence structuring. Additionally, in regard to my writing skills specifically, I learned to confirm name spellings via reliable sources and to cross-reference with other sources when necessary.

21

This same principle, I also apply to important
information I may include within a written piece
that may have conflicting opinions being
expressed about them at other sources. In these
cases, I will also include short quotes from
reputable sources, being careful to credit these
with a link to their online locations and the name
of the publishing entity or author. If I include
more than 50 words from a quoted source, it will
only be from those that allow reprinting or whose
information is clearly listed as being public
domain (non-copyrighted). In short, I have
improved my overall writing skills and techniques
as a result of my experience as topic editor for the
previously described content website, in spite of
my otherwise negative experiences with them.
Their required training for the position and my
ongoing article publishing for them were
admittedly positive aspects I gleaned from the
experience as well.

My experience with the website also led to my
publishing eBooks with major booksellers and my
inspiration for beginning this pursuit, was their
allowing of affiliate links to products related to
my editor topic.

I found on the website, where other topic editors were linking to books and eBooks they had written and this highly interested me. As a result, I began to format my articles into eBooks of my own and eventually, I also published these in paperback form. My sales of these type items have steadily grown and I am genuinely grateful for the fact that my experience with the website, though containing some negative aspects, led to these other opportunities for me. Due to my improved writing skills, the experience also resulted in my being accepted to write for another high-traffic, reputable multi-topic content website. I could actually view this experience as a series of steps up the ladder that led me toward a very satisfying degree of success for me as an aspiring author. With the fact that I am medically disabled and receiving social security disability as a result of multiple health issues, at my relatively young age of 50 years, the income I receive from my online publishing, especially the eBook projects, has been a genuine blessing.

It is my hope that my related experiences help to demonstrate to readers of the preceding headings, the fact that some negative online publishing events are bound to happen to us, when we pursue success as an author.

It is often our response to them that will determine their eventual outcome for us. We can allow them to hinder and to discourage us or we can see them as stepping stones that help to lead us into our eventual success.

8. Things I Recommend for Aspiring Authors Considering Content Website Work

When a writer is considering content websites as a beginning venue for developing their work, I recommend that they enter into agreements only with the more highly reputable sites, if at all possible. If you are not sure about a particular site's reputation regarding their treatment of writers, consider conducting a fairly extensive search online about the company in question. You might also consider finding a website's contact information, that lists the state they reside in and check with the Better Business Bureau (BBB) in that state, for any complaints that might be listed against them. Keep in mind that no complaints being listed does not necessarily indicate that they are a quality website to write for (i.e. newer websites and those who have resolved prior complaints). On the other hand, a small number of complaints does not necessarily indicate that they are a bad company to write for (i.e. those filed by former disgruntled employees and writers with bogus complaints). This can be valuable information however, when you add it into other information you may gather when you search online about a particular company.

Reading posts at writers forums that are indexed online, can also add to your search information about a content website. Here again, some gripes can be illegitimate but when you find many being posted that closely compare with each other, this might send up a red flag.

Some business information websites will list reviews for online companies that state how many employees they have, where they are located and what level of revenue they are generating. Keep in mind that websites, who make very little information available about their companies, may do so because they are hiding their intentions or because they want to be able to easily dissolve their assets should an investigation be launched against them. This also provides very little for online business-review websites to go on, in providing information about companies, to those conducting online searches.

I highly recommend that writers thoroughly read content contributor agreements/contracts offered by article publishing websites. Some arrangements offered by what some online sources refer to as "content farms", slight their writers/authors in regard to compensation for their work.

Some sites offer upfront payment only for submitted work that is approved for publishing but they do not offer ongoing revenue shares (residual income). Others may offer residual income but this will only cover ad revenue generated by visitors to their main website but it does not cover a provision for revenue shares to authors, generated by their extended marketing of articles (when placed on their sister sites or on other online content markets). I personally feel a content contributor agreement should include residual revenue-share income to writers, regardless of whether or not upfront payments for articles are also offered. I also believe writers should be covered in the terms of agreements, for all marketing a website performs with their articles, to exclude nothing that is earned from ad revenues, regardless of the extended content source that is generating it.

There is also the consideration an author should make in regard to the copyright terms a content website may require. Some of them ask for absolute exclusivity and this does not allow the author to republish their content elsewhere at a later date, should they decide to.

Writers vary in their preference regarding this term of agreement and many do not mind offering exclusivity, as long as the website publishing their articles is high-traffic and reputable.

It is important that content websites offer ongoing support to their writers. They should not feel slighted in the area of need for legitimate publishing issues to be resolved as promptly as possible (i.e. problems with a site's publishing tools or when they find an unauthorized website carrying their article, etc...).

When writers/authors feel they are being genuinely supported, they will be far more likely to continue with a content website. In many cases, websites accomplish this by not only having a support department but by also providing authors a support forum.

Lastly, the level of quality as reflected in a website's editing practices, is also a consideration for writers to make when considering entering into agreement with them. Some "content farms"; publish any and all articles submitted to them, with little or practically no editorial oversight.

This can mean that an author's work is going to be mixed-in with and surrounded-by very low quality content and this can reflect on the overall perception of a website by online visitors.

On the other hand, there is one particular content website conglomerate that will also remain nameless by me in this book that has such extremely strict editorial guidelines that they will actually screen-out highly experienced writers.

These type sites can make it nearly impossible for writers to publish numbers of articles over time, large enough to secure them a reasonable publishing income. In cases like these, you will often find posts being made on publisher's forums that are registering complaints regarding a website's overboard editorial requirements.

In short, there is reasonable balance that can be required by content websites in this area and this is also a major consideration for writers considering publishing work with them.

For a more extensive resource on the subject of online publishing for authors/writers, please see my related book/eBook titled: "Advice and Cautions for Independent Publishing Authors". I extend my most sincere Best Wishes to all of my fellow aspiring authors and thank you for reading what I hope will prove to be valuable information for you, as you move forward with your publishing efforts!

(END)

www.ingramcontent.com/pod-product-compliance
Lightning Source LLC
Chambersburg PA
CBHW071601170526
45166CB00004B/1752